Development of Art Therapy Application For Children

By : Koo, Jongsoon

TABLE OF CONTENTS

No.	TITLE	Page No.
1	**INTRODUCTION**	1
	1.1 Computer technology and mental health	2
	1.2 Digital Media and Art Therapy	4
	1.3 Children's Self-Esteem and Art Therapy	5
	1.4 Statement of the Problem	7
	1.5 Justification for the Study	8
2	**REVIEW OF LITERATURE**	10
	2.1 Overview of Art Therapy	10
	2.2 Theoretical Framework	11
	2.3 Digital Media and Computer Technology in Mental Health	11
	2.4 Digital Media in Art Therapy	13
	2.5 Digital Therapy and Children's Mental Health in India	15
	2.6 Children's Self-esteem and Art Therapy	17
3	**METHODS**	21
	3.1 Objective of the study	22
	3.2 Research design	22
	3.3 Procedure	22
	3.4 Hypothesis	34
	3.5 Operational Definition	34
	3.6 Sample and Sampling	35
	3.7 Instrument	36

	3.8. Data Analysis	36
	3.9 Ethical Consideration	36
4	**RESULTS**	**37**
	4.1 The result of Paired Sample t-test	**37**
	4.2 The result of Intervention for Each Session	38
	4.3. General Impression of the App from the School Counselors	52
5	**DISCUSSION**	55
	5.1 Development of an Art Therapy App, "Art about Me"	55
	5.2 Effectiveness of Art Therapy App for Children	56
6	**SUMMARY AND CONCLUSIONS**	**60**
	6.1 Major findings of the study	61
	6.2 Limitations of the Study	62
	6.3 Implications of the Study	62
7	**REFERENCES**	**64**
8	**APPENDICES**	**72**

Development and Effectiveness of an Art Therapy Application for Children

Art therapy is an integrative therapeutic form that uses art-making for anyone who needs the treatment to understand themselves, to cope with problems, and to enhance their quality of life. Engaging in creative art activities provide opportunities for individuals to improve mental health, cognitive ability, and sensory-motor skills. Non-verbal communication promotes self-expression for people who can't express their problems in words. Art therapy is used to develop interpersonal and communication skills, resolve conflicts, manage behavior and emotion, and enhance self-awareness and self-esteem (American Art Therapy Association [AATA], 2017; Buchalter, 2009; Wood, Molassiotis & Payne, 2011). Many researchers found effects of art therapy in clinical settings such as reducing depression and fatigue of cancer patients during chemotherapy treatment (Bar-Sela, Atid, Danos, Gabay, & Epelbaum, 2007) and anger and self-esteem of aggressive children (Alavinezhad, Mousavi and Sohrabi, 2014). Art therapy is also helpful in developing foundation skills in socialization and learning through art activities for children with Autism Spectrum Disorder (Gabriel, 2003).

Art therapy can be employed for people of all ages and with any issue. Techniques of art therapy are used by counselors, psychologists, social workers, psychiatrists, and art therapists (Malchiodi, 2003, p.1-3). Art therapy is particularly useful for children. Art is symbolic and non-verbal. Art provides an alternative way to communicate. It helps children understand themselves and safely express their emotions. Negative thoughts and feelings, fears, and wishes can be expressed in art (Rubin, 2010). Slayton, D'Archer and Kaplan (2010) reviewed art therapy studies from 1999 to 2007. Twenty-six of the thirty-five studies reviewed showed the effectiveness of art therapy on behavioral problems of children and adolescents. Child-centered art-making processes, confidentiality, and happy experience are essential in art therapy for children (Deboys, Holttum & Wright, 2016).

Drawing, painting, collages, clay, and play-dough are traditional art mediums. Pencils, markers, and crayons for drawing are familiar mediums from the pre-school age. Clients find it easy to express their thoughts and feelings in a comfortable environment. Painting gives freedom and flexibility to experiment with color and movement. Clients can experience texture and touch and use two- or three-dimensional materials through collages. Clay and play-dough are good mediums for using motor skills and helping people experiment with touch. In addition, puppets and masks, multimedia, and combining modalities such as music, movement, and art are used to express and communicate creatively. Computer technology is the new medium in art therapy intervention. After being familiar with the software, clients can enjoy it and express abstract images easily (Buchalter, 2009).

Computer technology and mental health

Computer technology and digital media are inextricably linked with modern human life. People can create a new production or a reproduction and share them with others by using a computer and the internet. In art, computer technology plays a significant role in producing and distributing art forms as well (Blythe, Light & O'Neill, 2007).

Digital media impacts not only human life but also medicine and mental health in the world. Health care professionals use computer technology to conduct online interventions and to communicate with people who have physical and mental limitations to approach a specific location for their health care. Computer-mediated psychotherapy, cyber-therapy, web-counseling, telehealth, telemedicine, e-therapy, telepsychiatry, and cyber-counseling have become new areas of research recently (Malchiodi, 2000, p14-15).

Some researchers found that technology is used to deal with learning disorders and psychological behavior change. Computer-assisted therapy was effective in scholastic skills for children with specific learning disorders in India (Vidyasagar & Kumar, 2013). Kraft, Schjelderup-Lund and Brendryen (2007) developed an individualized and interactive Digital Therapy Developer (DTD) to support behavioral change. It provided cost-effective personal therapy daily without having to meet therapists.

Fairburn and Patel (2016) explained the impacts of digital technology on the psychological treatment. Digital treatment is already used for individuals with depression, anxiety and insomnia. Interventions using digital technology were delivered via websites, smartphone apps or both. Digital technology was also used as means of administrating and interpreting assessment. A lot of questionnaires are available via a website or app and the program can score it and provide interpretation with reference. Digital training for therapists, clinicians and health workers is available too. The use of digital technology in treatment can impact public mental health service, community, and global dissemination. Researchers have suggested that digital treatment will be used more commonly soon. The systems of digital intervention need to be developed for their appropriate use.

In low- and middle- income countries, most individuals with mental health problems don't receive basic mental health care due to scarce mental health resources (Patel, 2007). There is a need to improve and invest in mental health care across the life span, and the public mental health system. Fu, Burger, Arjadi and Bockiting (2020) suggested that digital technology should be used to provide mental health services in low- and middle- income countries. Digital therapy was effective for individuals with mental health problems in low- resources countries. It can help bridge the mental health service gap for people with mental health issues because digital technology is increasing fast. Around 80% of the population have mobile phones, and half of the population can access the internet in low- and middle-income countries. Naslund, Shidhaye and Patel (2019) also reported that digital technology played an important role in supporting mental health services as tools for training, supervising, guiding treatment, and integrating services in low- income and middle- income countries.

India also has many digital media users, and they continue to increase (Statista Research Department, 2020). There are over 560 million internet users, and it was estimated that there would be around 600 million internet users by 2021. Active mobile social media users are 310 million, and it will increase to 400.3 million by 2021. Diwanji (2020) reported that most internet users used their mobile phones to access the internet due to low price mobile data and the growing number of smartphone users.

In primary care settings, smartphone apps are being used for some time now (Yellowlees & Chan, 2015). Mental health apps have also been developed to communicate between patients and mental health care providers, to provide therapy, interventions, or medication management, and to monitor their symptoms or behaviors. Non-specialist health workers have been using smartphone apps to develop skills and knowledge for providing mental health services in a rural setting (Naslund, Shidhaye & Patel, 2019).

The majority of the population in India is young and uses technology actively. India has experience in using telemedicine and electronic health care, including psychiatry. So mobile mental health care system would be a great solution to help people.

Digital Media and Art Therapy

Despite the development of computer technology and digital media, the use of technology has been controversial in art therapy. Art therapists' reasons for not using digital media in their therapy were the high cost of the devices, their unfamiliarity with the device, and their lack of interest (Peterson, Stovall, Elkins and Parker-bell, 2005). Orr's study (2006) also found that art therapists were not interested in using technology in their intervention. Above all, they believed that traditional art medium was more valuable and therapeutic than digital media.

However, it must be recognized that computer technology is a new creative tool that can be utilized in therapeutic settings (Thong, 2007). Computer is used as an important art medium for children and adolescents in school settings and hospitals. Digital art making process encompasses features of traditional art materials. Peterson (2010) also stressed that therapists could choose an art-making medium for their clients. Digital media has potential as an art therapy medium because it is already considered a standard tool in art therapy education and treatment. Kaimal, Rattigan, Miller and Haddy (2016) found that engagement with digital art media increased among adults. Digital art media was considered a significant therapeutic tool by art therapists for creating, sharing and consuming art. The Internet plays an important role in documenting, collaborating and sharing their creative artwork.

McLeod (1999) has addressed the benefits of digital art media in therapeutic interventions. Computer-assisted art therapy provides chances to improve the clients' creativity and ways to organize the artwork collection. There is no limitation for physical place and timing. Clients can feel free to express their emotions and thoughts with various tools and modify them anytime without any mark or stain. Even the price of the software is not high, and it is not difficult to learn how to use the program.

Digital art therapy also works effectively on children in various ways (Choe, 2017). Children aren't afraid of making mistakes while expressing their thoughts and feelings with the digital medium, which provides various options. They experience more flexibility and engagement than traditional papers. They can use digital media in the sessions without negative judgments, and therapeutic rapport is well established.

Choe (2014) studied art-making applications to suggest ideal features that satisfy art therapists and clients. Current art-making applications, called art apps, could not meet the needs of art therapists and clients. Those applications were developed not for therapeutic purposes but for creative art-making activities. It is important to create art therapy apps to satisfy the needs of practicing.

Some researchers have already developed software or an application for art therapy. Browne, Bederson, Druin, Sherman and Westerman (2000) designed a computer-based finger-painting program for education settings. Mattson (2015) developed a mobile application, "Art therapy draw!" for art therapy, based on two considerations of the art therapists: portfolio feature and security measures. However, various tools to express different images, mixed media capability, and the function of analyzing artwork still need to be developed.

Children's Self-Esteem and Art Therapy

Self-esteem refers to the individual's global evaluation of the self (Rosenberg, Schooler, Schoenbach & Rosenberg, 1995). Global self-esteem is an attitude toward the self as a whole, whereas specific self-esteem is an attitude to particular aspects. Global self-esteem is associated with psychological issues such as depression, anxiety, life satisfaction, happiness and negative affective states, while specific self-esteem is related to behaviors. Low self-esteem is related to problematic behaviors such as aggression, antisocial behavior and delinquency (Donnellan, Trzesniewski, Robins, Moffitt & Caspi, 2005). Self-esteem is clearly linked to a person's psychological condition.

Healthy self-esteem is an important factor for psychological stability, positive activity, and the psychological development of children (Hosogi, Okada, Fujii, Noguchi & Watanabe, 2012). Children's self-esteem is impacted by several factors such as family dysfunction, neighborhood, and schools. Children can overcome their low self-esteem when they experience positive achievements continuously. Hence it is important to evaluate self-esteem and support children in the school to understand children's past and present conditions and to deal with their psychological problems.

Early intervention is effective for children to build healthy and high self-esteem (Robins & Trzesniewski, 2005). Self-esteem is less stable during early childhood, which means self-esteem can be increased or decreased with ease. But it starts decreasing during adolescence and early adulthood. This is the reason why early intervention is significant to improve self-esteem for individuals. Self-esteem enhancement programs for children help them value themselves, others, and the world better. Dalgas-Pelish (2006) found that four lessons of self-esteem enhancement program were effective to improve self-esteem of 10 to 12-year-old children.

According to Shanmugam and Kathyayini (2017), adolescents who express themselves without psychological disturbance would have high self-esteem in India. There was a significant positive correlation ($rs= .64$) between assertive behavior and self-esteem among adolescents. Being able to express emotions and thoughts comfortably would be essential to improve self-esteem.

Art therapy is one of the effective interventions to improve self-esteem. Even people who have difficulty in verbal communication can express their feelings or images without pressure to talk. Hartz and Thick (2005) found that art therapy enhanced social relationship and self-esteem among female adolescents who had committed serious crimes. Participants experienced safety and comfort in self-expression that led to increased self-awareness and self-approval. They also were able to experience positive feelings such as success and pride, which they inculcated during the process of art activities.

Buchalter (2009) reported that using digital media as a tool in art therapy was beneficial to client's self-esteem improvement. Clients could learn how to use the program with ease and enjoy creating art by doing, changing, deleting and saving artwork with minimal efforts. They had choices and authority to create their own art work. A sense of control and artistic options of clients could enhance their self-esteem.

Although there are a lot of benefits of art therapy intervention, there is a paucity of art therapy studies in India. Prasad (2008) stated that even in art education setting, art curriculum or programs were insufficient due to the absence of training programs or books that help teachers. Limitation of traditional art mediums such as papers, crayons, color pencils, brush, paints, clay, etc., and the physical setting is a significant obstacle to provide art therapy in India.

Child and adolescent mental health services are also limited in India due to a lack of infrastructure and human resource development (Shastri, 2009). For sustained improvement in children's mental health, innovative and effective mental health services should be planned and implemented.

An art therapy application using digital media could be an alternative art medium in a therapeutic setting. It can replace the traditional art materials to overcome the limitation of it, especially in low- and middle- income countries like India. It is expected that the art therapy application would be useful to conduct art therapy anytime and anywhere for art therapists, school counselors, and special educators while maintaining confidentiality of the therapeutic setting.

Statement of the Problem

Based on the above literature, we can conclude that computer technology is used in various ways to support therapeutic service. Art therapy, a holistic and creative approach, is also adopting technology in communicating with clients, making art, sharing art forms, and intervention.

The usage of digital art media and the internet in art therapy is increasing now in creating, collaborating, and sharing artworks (Kaimal, Rattigan, Miller & Haddy, 2016). It has been found that digital art media has a lot of benefits and positive impacts on building therapeutic rapport, improving creativity, self- expression and self-esteem, and being flexible in any environment (Choe, 2017; McLeod, 1999; Thong, 2007).

But due to the absence of the art therapy software and application, art therapists use commercial art-making programs. Art therapists and clients are not satisfied with the confidentiality and security of these programs. Unfamiliarity with the device, absence of technology training for art medium to students or trainees of art therapy, disconnection from social interaction, and ethical issues are the main reason for art therapists not to use technology in their intervention as well.

In the Indian context, the physical environment does not meet the ideal setting for traditional art therapy or art education. It is not easy to provide traditional art mediums such as paper, pencil, crayon, paint, and brush, as art materials are expensive. Hence, taking into consideration all these aspects, there is a growing need to develop an art therapy application in India.

Justification for the Study

Art therapy is a holistic approach to help people explore and express themselves. It is effective to communicate with others, to improve wellbeing, and to relieve negative emotions. Art helps people express thoughts and emotions that people cannot express in verbal language. So, art therapy is a good option for young children. Through the art-making process, therapeutic rapport is well established as well (Malchiodi, 2007, p.12-17).

Health care professionals use computer technology for online interventions and to communicate with people who have physical and mental limitations to approach a specific location for their health care. Art Therapy has also begun to consider digital media a new medium in art therapy. Digital media can strengthen the therapeutic alliance between children and a therapist because the children can use digital media without judgment (Choe, 2017). Hesitation to create artwork is reduced as clients don't need specific skills to draw or paint the traditional way but instead can create any type of shape or line with various options (McLeod, 1999).

In India, mental health system is fragmented and uncoordinated (National Institute of Mental Health and Neuro-Sciences [NIMHAS], 2016). Lack of mental health experts, institutional care, and rehabilitation programs are the problems for providing mental health services effectively. Technology-based application is one of the highly recommended solutions to resolve the problem. Technology use is growing fast in India. The number of people using the internet and computer device is increasing rapidly. The use of digital art media is more convenient and easier than supplying traditional art materials. Developing an art therapy application can help by transcending space and time.

After the development of an app, it is important to examine the effectiveness of the app. Many researchers have already studied the effect of art therapy on self-esteem using traditional art mediums. The current study sought to determine the effect of art therapy using the application as a medium, on the self-esteem of children, thereby validating the effectiveness of the app. There is a need to develop an art therapy application to meet the expectation of mental health care. It is hoped that the development of an art therapy application will enable art therapists, school counselors, and special educators to provide art therapy in their session with ease.

Review of Literature

The purpose of this chapter is to provide a contextual review of the existing literature on art therapy, the use of digital media as a medium in art therapy practice for children, and the importance of self-esteem of children.

Overview of Art Therapy

Art therapy is a "powerful healing" to improve a person's wellbeing and daily life and experience therapeutic progress (Malchiodi, 2007, p.21-22). It is useful to develop a sense of self-awareness and to enhance emotional transformation.

There is ample research that supports the effectiveness of art therapy on various symptoms. Uttley, Stevenson, Scope, Rawdin and Sutton (2015) suggested that art therapy is an effective therapy for non-psychotic mental health problems such as depression, anxiety, and phobias. Foa (2009) also found that art therapy is useful to work with children who have experienced trauma. The art-making process is effective in accessing trauma-related experiences, and it provides opportunities to express children's internal thoughts and feelings using nonverbal language.

Nonverbal and creative art making is a safe way to approach children who are not able to express themselves effectively (Waller, 2006). It can help children explore and express their emotions. The visual art-making process provides opportunities for learning and an alternative way to communicate with others in positive ways. Children can transform their negative feelings into the object that they share with a therapist. It also helps children with ASD to improve communication skills, self-image, and learning skills (Schweizer, Kmorth & Spreen, 2014). Children became more flexible and relaxed at home and at school. They showed less anxiety and less anger while improving sensory and emotional regulation.

Children's artwork provides meaningful information about them (Lowenfeld & Brittain, 1987). Children's drawing shows their emotion, intellectual ability, and physical and social development. Also, children can learn through art activities. The process of art
making needs cognitive activity. Parents and teachers need to study children's drawings to understand them.

Theoretical Framework

Person centered approach, also known as Rogerian theory is based on his belief that people are trustworthy and they have own potential and capacity for self-understanding, personal growth and problem solving (Corey, 2013). The characters of the therapist and the client-therapist relationship are the essential factors for the therapeutic process. Congruence, unconditional positive regard and empathy are the most important part of the therapeutic relationship. Natalie Rogers, a daughter of Rogers, extended his theory to the person-centered expressive arts therapy. Drawing, painting, sculpting, movement, music and writing are used as artistic forms to express feelings, to get insights and to enhance personal growth.

Art therapy based on a person-centered approach provides clients opportunities to take meaningful and valuable action as well as to overcome their issues (Rogers, 2001). It is believed that an individual has the ability to develop toward growth and full potential. Expressed artwork from inner feelings or inner conflicts gives opportunities to facilitate self-awareness and healing. Art therapists should provide an empathic and congruent environment and unconditional positive regard. They trust their clients to find a way to express and develop their potential by themselves. Therapists have to respect clients' experiences and encourage them to share their stories and feelings to foster their creativity. Clients would find the ultimate destination. Without worrying about the beauty of the art, clients can gain insights into their deep feelings and thoughts that visual art helps to express.

Art therapy can provide opportunities for clients to express their feelings with various materials and to be aware of their emotions. It helps them to gain insights and to find the solution for their problems. Especially, children who could have difficulties to express their thoughts or feeling can feel free to express. Art is an enjoyable activity for children. The role of the therapist is to provide the materials and a warm environment for children to be able to aware of their emotion and utilizing their potential.

Digital Media and Computer Technology in Mental Health

As computer users are increasing, more concerns and issues are being raised. Especially for children, the effects of using computers are very complicated.

Subrahmanyam, Kraut, Greenfield and Gross (2000) reviewed articles to understand the effects of home computer use among children. Some studies found there were negative impacts on physical wellbeing such as obesity, seizures, and hand injuries. Playing violent computer games influence aggressive behaviors among children. Using the internet for a long time was related to increases in depression.

On the other hand, some studies showed that computer games with rapid movement, interaction, and imagery influenced visual intelligence skills positively. Moreover, the computer has become an important educational source these days. The use of home computers is linked to better academic performance. Therefore, the amount of time spent, type of activity, and the contents should be considered and managed while using computers to benefit.

Hind and Sibbald (2015) identified the benefits of smartphone applications in mental health. Firstly, patients and doctors experienced the usability and functionality of apps. It was also helpful for doctors to understand their patients' condition and to communicate with them. Secondly, people preferred to use applications and were willing to use them more frequently. Thirdly, the application was useful to monitor patients' symptoms accurately. Fourthly, psychological interventions such as cognitive-behavioral therapy, dialectical behavioral therapy, and acceptance and commitment therapy were applied to smartphone applications. Fifthly, there was a positive impact on clinical outcomes such as depression, anxiety, stress, and so on. Finally, the application could allow many people to access mental health care. For successful results, the application must be individualized and include adaptive learning. Feedback, professional counselor support, and technical support were important factors too. Long-term adherence and confidentiality were barriers to using an application.

Certain ethical issues of online therapy should be considered in a clinical setting: confidentiality, identification, electronic storage of records, and the online therapeutic relationship (Malchiodi, 2000). Secure websites or encryption technology have to be used if one is using the internet to communicate with clients. Limits of confidentiality should be informed to clients, and the data also should be managed carefully.

Identification is also one of the issues in online therapy. Sometimes, it is not possible to verify the actual therapist when they use online communication. So, therapists who work online should provide professional information such as certification, education, and professional history.

In terms of recording the communication, an encryption system should be used. Unintentionally, the soft copy could be saved or erased very easily. The data has to be saved in hard drives, and back-up copies also should be made regularly. If transferring confidential information to authorized parties, it should be sent via a secure system with clients' permission.

To build an online therapeutic relationship, the therapist should determine the feasibility of online therapy for each client. Limitations and advantages of online therapy should be explained to the clients. If online therapy is not suitable for the client, the therapist should inform an alternative therapy. An alternative way of communication and other professional contacts should be provided to the clients for any unexpected situation.

Digital Media in Art Therapy

Malchiodi (2000) has introduced art therapists who have used technology in art therapy sessions earlier. In 1985, Diane Weinberg used computers in the treatment of people with physical limitations such as quadriplegia, stroke, or brain trauma. She found that patients were comfortable in using a computer because specific art skills were not required while creating their artworks. Devorah Samet Canter used technology with children and adolescents with emotional disturbances in her art therapy sessions in 1989. They used computers to create images while expressing their emotions and fantasies. It helped them tell their problems. It also gave opportunities to develop their self-esteem by learning computer graphic programs. Hartwich and Brandecker also used a computer painting program for their patients with mental illness such as schizophrenia in their art therapy intervention in 1993. They found that ease of computer-based painting decreased the fear. It was also useful and easy to store the progress of patients' artwork and to review them.

Even though digital media's effects and benefits in art therapy are well known, usage of it in sessions is still lower than general usage. Orr's research in 2006 found the art therapists' reasons for not using technology in sessions, which included: expensive devices, a lack of value in their agencies, time constraints for use and training, discomfort with the technology, and the idea that digital media didn't meet the clients' sensory needs.

With time, the use of technology by the general public has increased. Orr's study in 2012 showed that the use of technology by art therapists had also increased, and art therapists' understanding of technology had changed. But training in the use and ethics of digital media for art therapists still needed to be developed.

Kaimal, Rattigan, Miller and Haddy (2016) reported that the number of people who use digital media for art-making and art sharing increased in general. Art therapists already used digital media in their therapy, and they could combine traditional art media with computer technology. Especially with young people who were familiar with technology, digital media was effective in building a therapeutic relationship. Digital art-making was also helpful for a depressed and reluctant adolescent with OCD to express his feelings and control them. To use digital media for creating and sharing art in a therapeutic setting, students and trainees of art therapy need to understand digital media as an art therapy tool. They need to be educated about the skills and ethics of digital media such as copyright, confidentiality, and the advantages and disadvantages of using technology as a therapeutic media.

These days, the use of digital technology has grown rapidly around the world. Using technology in a clinical setting is inevitable. Digital media has already become an alternative media in art therapy (McLeod, 1999; Orr, 2006; Thong, 2007).

Choe (2017) studied the benefits of using digital art media in the intervention. Young clients experienced the freedom to use digital media without judgment, so the use of digital media was effective in strengthening the therapeutic alliance. Clients could also experience control and freedom over their work without the fear of making mistakes and were free to use their cognitive and creative skills. They had various options to choose from, such as types of canvas or pressure-sensitive stylus. Convenience, forming a healthy habit, self-assessment, and self-monitoring were the additional advantages.

Barber and Garner (2017) introduced several art therapy apps in their book.

They explored that artwork made by art-making apps was similar to ones made in traditional ways such as painting, coloring, or drawing. The Art therapist has to take responsibility for using apps in the intervention and confidentiality, and ethical issues have to be strictly considered.

But there are no art therapy apps that can be used in clinical settings (Choe, 2014). Existing art apps developed for commercial use didn't meet the needs for therapeutic purposes. Art therapy app must include various options to create art and immediate responsiveness of control for easy and simple operation. The function of the art therapist's control over the apps, portfolio, recording the art-making process, a digital library such as sticker, and confidentiality must be included.

When developing software to be used in a clinical setting, it should be designed by therapists and used under the guidance of therapists (Matthews, Doherty, Coyle & Sharry, 2008). It has to have a locking system to protect data that others should not access to meet the ethical consideration. This software can be implemented by clients easily, and technical support must be provided.

Mihailidis et al. (2010) developed art therapy applications that had three different types of software based on survey results for adults with dementia. The system embodied the ideas: focusing on paintings and drawings that adults with dementia liked the most, enabling users to self-select activities, and adding the option of co-work with art therapists.

Mattson (2015) developed a mobile application, "Art therapy draw!" for art therapy, based on two considerations of the art therapists, portfolio feature, and security measures. There is a save icon to organize the clients' artwork. Art therapists or clients can set up a password to save their art images and to maintain confidentiality. It was easy to operate the application in drawing, setting up a password, and saving images in a secure folder. However, various tools to express different images, mixed media capability, and the function of analyzing artwork have to be developed.

Digital Therapy and Children's Mental Health in India

According to Shastri (2009), approximately 50 million Indian children have mental health problems. 10 % of children aged between five to fifteen years have a mental health disorder. The prevalence of mental disorders among children aged 13-17 years was 7.3% and it was similar in both genders (NIMHANS, 2016). Around 9.8 million children needed active mental health interventions. The prevalence of mental illness among urban children was nearly double compared to rural children. The most common mental health problems were Depressive disorder (2.6%), Agoraphobia (2.3%), Intellectual Disability (1.7%), Autism Spectrum Disorder (1.6%), Anxiety disorder (1.3%), and Psychotic disorder (1.3%). This survey also reported a huge treatment gap for mental illness, and mental health services were low prioritized. Malnutrition and anemia lead to growth retardation in 30 % of unborn babies. Deprivation, discrimination, and economic, sexual, or educational exploitation that children experience all through life can cause poor identity and self-worth.

Despite a large number of children and adolescents who need mental health services, nearly 90 % of children with a mental disorder don't receive any mental health service due to lack of infrastructure and human resource development (Shastri, 2009). India lacks a comprehensive policy, mental health system, and programs for children and adolescents.

The environment and setting for art therapy or art education in India are also very limited (Prasad, 2008, p. 81). It is not easy to set an ideal physical environment such as lighting, water supply, and calm space for art therapy. Especially in school, there are many students in the classroom, and facilities are not sufficient.

According to Naslund, Aschbrenner, Araya, Marsch, Unützer, Patel and Bartels (2017), digital technology effectively supports the clinical care and management of mental health care, and for providing mental health training and education to health workers in low-income and middle-income countries. Particularly, it might be an effective method for young people aged 10 to 24 years to address their mental health needs. In low resource settings where people with a mental disorder can hardly receive the mental health care due to the underdeveloped health care system and lack of mental health specialists and treatment opportunities, technology could help people access mental health care for their wellbeing.

Malhotra, Chakrabarti and Shah (2019) also suggested that digital technology could play an important role in delivering effective mental health care in the low- and middle-income countries. Due to the dearth of resources, there are limitations to provide mental health care to rural areas or remote sites. Innovative digital mental health care system can support mental health care services effectively in resource deficient countries like India. However, the use of non-smartphones and different languages were obstacles to using mental health apps for patients with mental illnesses and their caregivers in India (Deb et al., 2018). Their opinions and suggestions should be considered when apps are developed to solve the problems and support patients and their caregivers.

Digital art therapy can be conducted anywhere and anytime without extra effort, such as preparing traditional art materials or cleaning up (McLeod, 1999). The most significant benefit of it is that clients don't need to have specific art skills. Clients can create any lines and shapes with various tools: brush strokes, airbrush, and so on. Even if children are not confident about art skills due to the absence of learning art before, they can try different tools to create their artwork and modify them anytime without any mark or stain. Their artwork can be saved in stages, copied, shared, and stored. It is believed that digital art therapy can provide effective psychological service in India.

Children's Self-esteem and Art Therapy

For children and adolescents, self-esteem plays a significant role in their psychological wellbeing. Many researchers studied the self-esteem of children and adolescents in school settings.

It is essential to distinguish global self-esteem from specific self-esteem (Rosenberg, Schooler, Schoenbach & Rosenberg, 1995). Global self-esteem is associated with psychological wellbeing, whereas specific self-esteem is more related to better behavior and academic performance. So, these two types of self-esteem cannot be used interchangeably. It is necessary to understand the nature of global and specific self-esteem to design and provide appropriate interventions. Rosenberg Self-Esteem Scale was developed to measure global self-esteem.

Self-esteem changes across the entire life span (Robins, Trzesniewski, Tracy, Gosling & Potter, 2002). Self-esteem is increased by the self-verification process, which occurs when group-based identities match the meanings in their identities (Cast & Burke, 2002). Social groups and relationships influence Self-verification that is a personal process. If individuals fail to verify their identities constantly, their self-esteem decreases, and individuals become more vulnerable to negative impacts.

Rosenberg Self-Esteem Scale has been used to measure children's self-esteem in the Indian context. To examine the effects of self-esteem in children with Dyslexia aged between eight to fourteen years, Rosenberg Self-Esteem Scale was administered (Jesna & Edward, 2014). It was also used to study self-esteem and academic achievement of urban and rural students aged 12 to 14 years in Varanasi District, India (Joshi & Srivastava, 2009).

According to Rosenberg, Schooler, and Schoenbach (1989), self-esteem is associated with psychological symptoms and depression. They studied the relationship between self-esteem and adolescent problems, juvenile delinquency, poor school performance, and depression, and the relationship was bidirectional.

There is a strong relationship between global self-esteem and problematic behaviors (Donnellan, Trzesniewski, Robins, Moffitt & Caspi, 2005). Low self-esteem was positively related to aggression, antisocial behaviors, and delinquency. Moreover, self-esteem could predict aggression in the future.

Lee, Park and Jang (2017) found that self-esteem and happiness were positively correlated among elementary, middle, and high school students. Self-esteem and school violence victimization were correlated negatively. Self-esteem was partially mediated between school violence victimization, and happiness. It was suggested that self-esteem enhancing programs, along with a school violence prevention program, could improve students' happiness and wellbeing at school. Ateerah and Lukman (2019) also supported the finding that self-esteem and happiness are correlated positively. Self-esteem was negatively correlated with depression. Sukumaran, Vickers, Yates and Garralda (2003) also found lower global self-esteem among children and adolescent psychiatric patients. They had psychological problems such as anxiety, depression, conduct disorder, and hyperkinetic disorder.

Dhillon, Dhawan, Ahuja, A, and Papneja (2016) studied factors that shape the self-esteem of adolescent girls in India. They found that academic self-efficacy, relationship with peers, physical appearance / body image, family conflict, gender discrimination and social comparison were linked with self-esteem.

According to Shanmugam and Kathyayini (2017), improving assertiveness, such as acting in their best interest without anxiety or expressing feelings or thoughts comfortably, would help enhance their self-esteem. Malik and Varghese (2020) also supported that assertiveness training was effective and cost-effective to improve adolescents' self-esteem in India.

Many researchers studied the effects of art therapy on self-esteem. Art therapy is an effective intervention to improve children's self-esteem (AATA, 2017; Buchalter, 2009; Wood, Molassiotis & Payne, 2011).

Alavinezhad, Mousavi and Sohrabi (2014) studied that children with aggressive behavior improved their self-esteem and reduced their anger after the art therapy intervention. Group art therapy enhanced self-esteem and reduced aggressiveness and behavior problems among adolescents who received probation orders due to delinquency (Lee, 2016; Mun & Hong, 2015). Art therapy intervention gave them opportunities to look back on their past and to introspect within themselves. It also led them to hope for their future. They were able to express their negative emotions safely.

Richards et al. (2018) found that visual arts education programs including hat decoration, collage, embossing, painting, ceramics, photography, and printmaking for eight weeks, effectively enhanced self-esteem among people with Alzheimer's disease and related dementias. Through this art education program, they could experience a sense of accomplishment, which could lead to improved self-esteem, and learn concentration, visual-spatial skills, organization, and sensory-motor skills, which could be used in daily life.

Although there is a dearth of academic research work on art therapy in India, few studies proved the effects of art therapy for children in the Indian setting. WCCL Foundation (2013) reported that Art Based Therapy (ABT) was beneficial to children at risk and children with special needs in India. Nearly 75% of children with special needs, including Cerebral palsy, Intellectual and development disorder, Autism spectrum disorder (ASD), Pervasive development disorder, Learning disability, and

ADHD made a positive shift in expression, body motor skills, and cognition. Art-making activities such as drawing, painting, cutting, exercises, and music, enhanced body coordination, and muscle tone. They also were able to express their feelings and communicate with others while creating art expression. Koo and Thomas (2019) also found that art therapy was effective for children with ASD in India. There was progress in the developmental art stages and cognition, social skills, and motor skills improved.

According to the literature, the use of computer technology is increasing rapidly in communication, workspaces, education, and mental health service. In art therapy intervention, a digital application can be used effectively to provide therapeutic services to children. In resource deficient countries, it would play a significant role to provide effective mental care service. Due to the absence of an art therapy application, the needs of art therapists and clients are not satisfied yet. They require an application that maintains the confidentiality of client information and the function of therapists' control over the process. These studies supported the need for an art therapy application to be developed in collaboration with an art therapist and software developer to satisfy the needs of art therapists and clients.

Methods

This research aimed to develop an art therapy app as a new tool to provide effective mental health services to children, especially in low resource settings. In art therapy intervention, basic art materials are needed, such as pencils, crayons, or markers for drawing, watercolors, tempera, brushes, and finger paints for painting, clay, play-dough, yarn, felt, wood, papers, etc. A space that has good lighting, storage for art materials, and artwork are needed as well. Water supply is also an essential element for the setting for art therapy. But in low resource contexts such as schools in India's rural areas, it isn't easy to get art materials and space not only for the therapy but also for the art class. An art therapy app could be a solution to provide art therapy materials and to bridge the mental health gap. Recently, digital media usage has been on the rise globally, and the use of digital technology in clinical settings is also increasing. It is thought that the development and usage of digital media in art therapy can meet the needs of the time.

The research was carried out in two stages: First, an art therapy app was developed as a medium to replace traditional art materials, and secondly, art therapy for self-esteem intervention using the app was conducted by school counselors to examine the effectiveness of the app as an alternative art medium in art therapy.

The first stage had two phases. In the first phase the app was developed by an art therapist and a technical team. In the second phase, training on the use of the app was given to school counselors. Feedback was taken, and modifications to the app were also made.

In the second stage, three school counselors conducted art therapy intervention for enhancing self-esteem in three different schools. They dealt with children who had various kinds of problematic issues at school. Literature has shown that children's self-esteem is linked with their psychological wellbeing, happiness, and problematic behaviors. To help children cope with their issues, art therapy for improving self-esteem was designed and provided to children.

The Institutional Ethics Committee of Christ (Deemed to be University) approved this study. Permission to conduct the research was also gained from the participants, school authorities, and parents in the second stage.

Objective of the study

The objective of the study was to develop an art therapy app for a smartphone or a tablet suitable for art therapy intervention and to examine the effectiveness of an art therapy app as an alternative art medium through an art therapy intervention for children's self-esteem

Research design

To achieve the objectives of the study, there were three phases for main investigation.

Figure 1

Three phases for main investigation

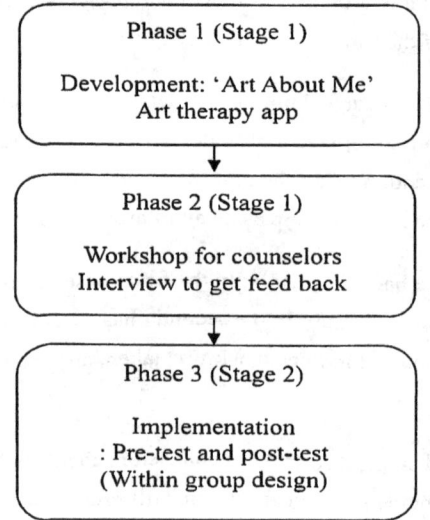

Procedure

Phase 1. The researcher designed an Art therapy app for a smartphone and tablet. The researcher is a certified art therapist with the Korean Art Psychotherapy Association. A developer from the Centre for Digital Innovation at Christ (Deemed to be University) provided technical assistance for the app. The app was developed according to the manual that was provided by the researcher. This is an Android app for free download.

The name of the app is "Art about Me." Some researchers had already given suggestions to develop a software for therapeutic settings (Browne, Bederson, Druin, Sherman & Westerman, 2000; Choe, 2014; Matthews, Doherty, Coyle, & Sharry, 2008). The researcher, who is an art therapist and understands the core elements of an art therapy app, designed this app to meet the ideal characteristics of the app. The technical features of this app are as follows.

- Confidentiality, privacy, and security: After installing the application, the therapist can register as an administrator. Clients can create their accounts with their name and password. Only administrators can access data, the list of clients, and their drawings with time order. Ethical principles such as confidentiality, privacy, and security were mainly considered while designing the app (Substance Abuse and Mental Health Services Administration, 2015). The app was developed to protect children's drawings and their data from being accessed without authorization, and to comply with technology tools' ethical considerations.

- Backing up system: The administrator can back up the data in the SD card of the device. Only with admin ID, data can be exported and backed up when the app is newly installed.

- Making journal: After completing artwork, clients can save their work with a title, comments, and date. They can make their own portfolio with their journal.

- Ease of use: With little guidance from the instructor, it is easy to log-in, to use, and to make a journal of clients. Drawing, taking pictures, and editing are easy to use.

- Digital accessories: Emotion stickers, taking photos, and editing are available.

- Non-internet-based app: Once the app is installed, internet access is not needed to use the program.

Phase 2. After developing the app, two days intensive training workshop was conducted for school counselors and a teacher. The workshop participants were members of a psychotherapeutic center, which provided professional psychological services, especially school counseling, in Bengaluru. One teacher and seven school counselors participated in the workshop. They were interested in art as a therapeutic form and already used art in their counseling interventions. At the beginning of the study, they showed a great passion for participating in the workshop to study art therapy. They already had children's artwork that they wanted to discuss with an expert. Time for exploring the children's artwork was arranged during the workshop at the request of school counselors. After the workshop, the researcher and participants communicated via email and smartphone messenger when participants had questions.

The school counselors had a list of children from their respective schools who needed counseling support. Teachers had referred these children to the counselors due to various issues such as bullying, academic issue, or behavior problems in the classroom. Table 1 shows the children's presenting feelings as perceived by the teachers and the school counseling team. Some of the children had multiple problems and emotional issues. It seemed to be related to low self-esteem. School counselors and teachers agreed to conduct a self-esteem enhancing program using art therapy.

Table 1

Children's presenting feelings

Presenting feelings	Number of children who experienced these feelings
Feeling inferior to others	1
Feeling inferior to others in studies	5
Feeling inferior to others in appearance	5
Feeling low	4
Feeling disturbed	1

| Feeling sad | 2 |
| Feeling angry | 1 |

The Workshop included Basic art therapy, an introduction to 'Art about Me,' and seven sessions of art therapy intervention to improve children's self-esteem. The workshop contents were designed based on art therapy books (Koh, Yoo, Lee, Lee, Beak, Lee & Jung, 2012; Lowenfeld & Brittain, 1987; Rubin, 2010).

On the first day of the workshop, basic art therapy was introduced to participants, including the definition of art therapy, characteristics of art materials, children's drawing and the developmental stages in art, and two art-based assessments. The House-Tree-Person (H-T-P) test and the Kinetic Family Drawing (K-F-D) test are projective tests (Burns, 2009). In the HTP test, a client is asked to draw a house, tree, and person on separate pieces of paper. The drawings are interpreted to assess the client's personality and cognitive, emotional, and social functioning. The KFD test asks a client to draw his / her family doing something. These two drawing tests can give a certain amount of information about individuals and their families. The participants were interested in art therapy as they already used art in their counseling sessions when children were reluctant to talk about their stories. They collected all children's work and brought it to the workshop to discuss their artwork and the case.

On the second day, the art therapy app, "Art about Me" was introduced. Participants learned how to use the app and learned how to conduct a self-esteem enhancement art therapy intervention. After experiencing the app, they gave feedback to the researcher to upgrade the app.

The sessions of self-esteem improvement intervention (see *table 2*) were designed by the researcher based on the previous studies about art therapy for improving self-esteem and a book about art therapy techniques and was also supervised by an expert art therapist (Buchalter, 2009; Lee, 2016; Mun & Hong, 2015). This intervention was designed to be conducted and completed within one academic term. The sessions were planned taking into consideration the school calendar, mid-term and final exams, holidays, and school events. Brief contents of the workshop are as follows:

> Workshop – Day 1
> - What is Art therapy?
> - Understanding Art Materials
> - Understanding children's drawing and developmental stages in Art
> - Art-based assessment: HTP test, KFD test
> - Case study: Interpretation and progress of the children's artwork
>
> Day 2
> - Understanding Art Therapy App and how to use 'Art about Me'
> - Seven sessions of Art therapy intervention on self-esteem for children were introduced. Details are as below.

Table 2

Seven sessions of Art therapy intervention on self-esteem for children

Session	Topic	Procedure / Goals
1	Introduction: Art about me Free drawing	The client becomes familiar with the application through free drawing. In the warm atmosphere, he/she expresses his/her emotion and thoughts.
2	Self-portrait	Using a camera and emotion stickers of app, the client takes a selfie and edits it. Goals include enhancing self-awareness and self-esteem by the exploration of self, facial expression, emotion, and understanding his/her interests, personality, strength, and weakness.
3	Body scan (Soothing music will be given)	In the beginning, clients close their eyes and relax his/her body parts with deep breaths. After body image scanning, the client takes a full body picture and decorates the body and background.

		Goals include learning how to relax the body, understanding the beauty of the body, and appreciating the body.
4	Draw myself as a superhero	At the beginning of the session, various superheroes such as Superman, Spiderman, and Wonder-woman are discussed. The client would draw himself/herself as a superhero focusing on characters, strengths, and powers. After drawing, discuss why he/she chooses the character and what strengths and power can help others. Explore if there are some similarities between a superhero and the client. Goals include enhancing self-awareness and self-esteem by exploring his/her strengths.
5	The happiest moment & saddest moment	The client thinks about the happiest and saddest moments they had before and draw them. Through this process, the client can explore his/her thoughts, emotions, and behaviors that influence his/her day. Goals are increasing awareness of the factors that impact life and learning how to balance the good and bad they face.
6	The first smile	Ask the client to draw the first person who smiled at him/her or brought a smile to his/her face. Help the client remember the person and express appreciation to people. Goals include learning to appreciate people

		and having a positive perspective to see the world.
7	Yourself in the future	Instruct the client to draw him/her self after 10 and 20 years. Encourage the client to think and to draw in detail: family, friend, name card, and costume related to a job in the future. Goals include giving opportunities to think of self in positive ways and in detail. While hoping for the future, intervention is terminated.

Tablet pcs with the app were distributed to school counselors during the workshop, and they learned how to use the app and practiced it. As app users, school counselors gave feedback on the app to upgrade the app as below, and the app was revised based on it. This process ensured the validity of the app.

Table 3 shows the details of the feedback from the school counselors and the solutions given by the researcher and developer of this study.

Table 3

Feedback and Solution

Feedback from counselors	Solution
Redo / undo function needed.	Redo/undo developed.
After selecting brush types, it will be useful to show which brush is selected.	Applied.
Pixel size is too big to draw details.	Varied brush size from 1 to 99
Is it possible to use a stylus?	Finger drawing is available. In case the device has a stylus, it will work.
Backing up system -Is it possible that two data can be merged? -Can we import data into existing app without uninstalling and reinstalling?	Data can be exported at any time, but only when the app is installed, data can be imported. Currently, it is not possible for two data to be merged.

The functions of the revised app, 'Art about Me' is as follows. After installing the app, the instructor can create his/her account. This is the most important part of the app because it strengthened confidentiality, privacy and security of the app. Only the instructor can open the client's drawings with his ID and password. It also shows the backing up system of the app. If there is previous data which was exported before, the instructor can select a data file and restore it when he/she installs the app. In case the instructor wants to change the device due to any reasons, he/she can save the data and export it to restore in another device (see *Figure 1*).

Figure 2

Open page: The instructor's account and backing up system

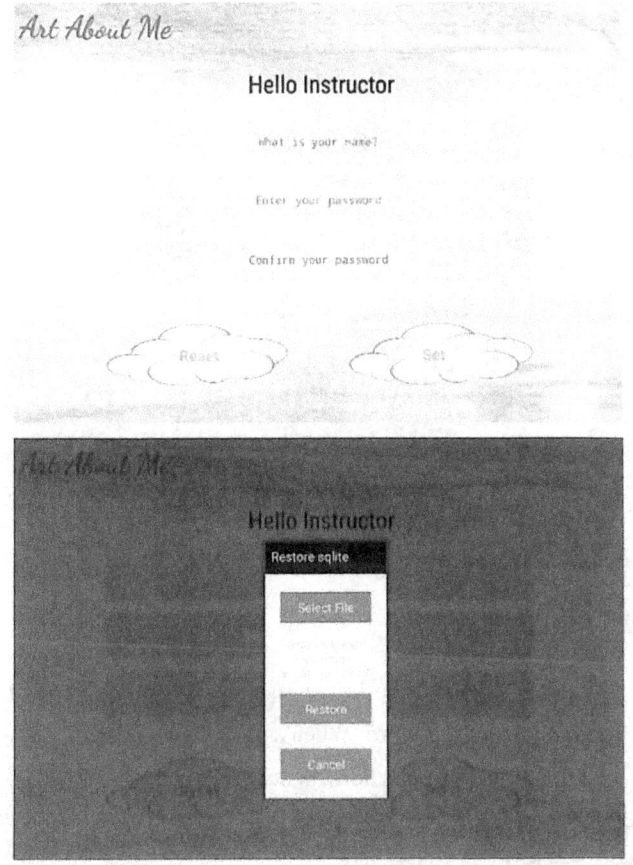

Only after the instructor's setting can clients get an opportunity to create their account to participate in the art therapy intervention. It will be under the supervision of the therapist. There is no limit to the number of accounts. Figure 2 shows how to restore the backup data when the instructor installs the app.

Figure 3

Client registration page

After the instructor's registration, clients can register the app. They have to access the app with their ID and password. When a new client creates the account, he/she will click the left button 'Register for Clients.' After creating their own account, he/she can click the right button 'start' to use the app. Then the client can see the login page to put in his ID and password.

Figure 4

Start (Login) page & main drawing page

After the client logs in, he/she can see the white canvas with icons indicating each function. The client can draw on a tablet with fingers and use drawing functions such as brush, eraser, colors, and camera with ease. Basic drawing function, selecting brush size and eraser size, taking pictures and editing, coloring, redo / undo, decoration with stickers are available (see *Figure 4*).

After completing a drawing, they can save their drawings with dates and comments about their work. Each drawing can be saved and listed in order. It helps therapists document clients' progress. The clients can see their journal by saving their artwork (see *Figure 5*).

Figure 5

Save

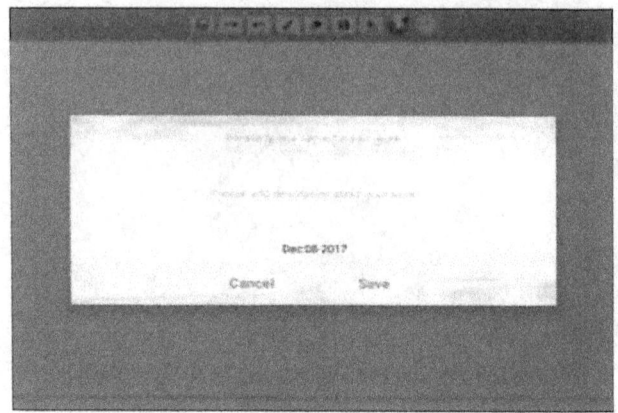

Only the therapist who has an instructor's ID and password can open the list of clients and their work. When the art therapist logs into the app, he/she can see the client list. If he/she clicks on the name of the client, he/she can see the drawing list of the client. It is easy to document clients' drawings with date and comments (see *Figure 6*).

Figure 6

List of clients and list of drawing

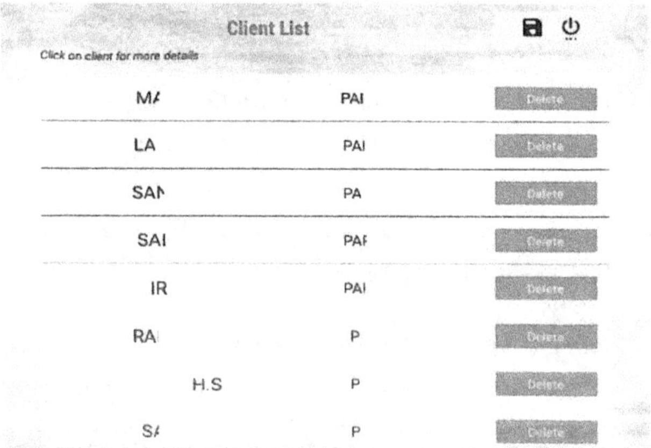

Finally, the client's drawing is shown with the topic and comments after clicking the drawing name. Therapists can see the progress of the client, and the client can review their drawings and the past. (see *Figure 7*).

Figure 7

Client's drawing

'Art about Me' would meet the needs of therapists and clients. It is easy to use for children and has various options. Confidentiality, privacy, security, making journal/documentation, and backing up system are included for use in a clinical setting.

The app is not a game, and the client can use the app only under the guidance of the therapist for therapy purposes. Therefore, there is no concern over any sort of addiction to the app.

Phase 3. In the implementation phase, art therapy using the app as a medium was conducted for 16 children by three school counselors in different schools. Among seven school counselors who participated in the art therapy workshop in phase two, three school counselors who have more than two-year experience joined the study for the final phase. They worked at different schools, and students were referred to them by class teachers for counseling and therapy. Following the approval from the Institutional Review Board (IRB), permission was obtained from schools, and informed consent was collected from parents and assent from children.

In school settings, school counselors deal with various emotional and psychological problems of children. Global self-esteem is highly associated with psychological symptoms such as depression, anxiety, and life satisfaction. Children's self-esteem can be enhanced effectively by early intervention, and it is related to children's psychological conditions. Enhanced self-esteem would affect children's daily life at school and home positively. Especially in this study, school teachers and the counseling team found children feeling inferior, feeling low, feeling disturbed, feeling sad, and feeling angry. Hence, self-esteem was focused on in this study, and Rosenberg's self-esteem scale was used to measure global self-esteem. After one week of the pre-test, school counselors used the art therapy app in their school counseling sessions with their clients. One week after the intervention, the post-test of children's self-esteem was measured with Rosenberg's self-esteem scale.

Hypothesis

There is no improvement in self-esteem in children after the art therapy intervention using the art therapy app, 'Art about Me.'

Operational Definition

App. App refers to "an application for a mobile phone" (Merriam-Webster, 2019). In this study, an android application for a tablet pc was developed by the researcher and a developer from the Center for Digital Innovation (CDI) in Christ University.

Self-esteem. In this study, self-esteem refers to "the individual's positive or negative attitude toward the self as a totality." It is a general feeling of self-worth (Rosenberg, Schooler, Schoenbach & Rosenberg, 1995).

Sample and Sampling

The population of the present research is children belonging to the age group of eight to fifteen. A representative sample of 16 children was chosen by using purposive sampling. These children were referred by teachers due to their problems such as bullying, academic problem, or behavioral problem at schools. They were students from three different government schools with English medium education.

Inclusion criteria. Inclusion criteria are as below.
1. Children between the age ranges of eight to fifteen took part in the study.
2. Children were the clients of school counselors who have undergone the art therapy training workshop.

Exclusion criteria. Exclusion criteria are as below.
1. Children identified with Autism spectrum disorder, mental retardation, and developmental disorders by school records.

2. Children who were under counseling other than the current art therapy intervention.

Table 4 showed the age of the sample in the present study.

Table 4

Age of the sample (N=16)

	N	Mean Age
Male	11	11.6
Female	5	12.6

Sample size was sixteen. Eleven boys and five girls participated in this study. Mean age of boys was 11.6 and mean age of girls was 12.6. These students were chosen by school teachers and counseling team from three different schools. Three, five and eight students were selected from each school. They hadn't undergone any other therapy or counseling other than art therapy.

Instrument

Self-esteem was assessed pre and post the intervention to determine the effectiveness of the art therapy app for children.

Rosenberg Self-Esteem Scale. Rosenberg self-esteem scale, developed by Morris Rosenberg in 1965, is a ten-item scale for measuring stable sense of personal worth. It is a four-point Likert scale format which contains positive and negative questions ranging from strongly agree to strongly disagree. The higher scores indicate greater levels of self-esteem. According to Rosenberg (1965), internal consistency ranged from 0.77 to 0.88 and test-retest reliability ranged from 0.82 to 0.85. Criterion validity was 0.55.

The Rosenberg self-esteem questionnaire has been used in earlier studies in India with Indian adolescents aged twelve to fourteen (Joshi & Srivastava, 2009) and Dyslexic children aged eight to fourteen (Jesna & Edward, 2014).

Data Analysis

A paired sample t-test was used to analyze children's self-esteem in phase three. Content analysis was used to analyze the art therapy intervention.

Ethical Consideration

- Theory and practical training of art therapy were provided to counselors who participated in this research.
- Informed consent was obtained from parents and assent from children prior to the study.
- Confidentiality was strictly maintained.
- The physical and psychological health of the participants during the study was taken care of by teachers and school counselors from the psychotherapeutic center.
- After the completion of this study, counselors continued to give individual counseling to the children.
- On requests by the participants, the results of the study were debriefed to them.

Results

Three school counselors conducted art therapy intervention using the app "Art about Me" to 16 children. Before and after the intervention, self-esteem was measured to explore the effects of art therapy with the app. IBM SPSS statistics 20.0 version was used for analyzing the data. The analysis of the results is presented below.

The Results of Paired Sample t-test

Table 5

Tests of Normality

differences	Kolmogorov-Smirnov			Shapiro-Wilk		
	Statistic	df	Sig.	Statistic	df	Sig.
	.202	16	.082	.936	16	.301

Before conducting a paired sample t-test, the normality of data was tested. Table 5 indicates that differences in scores for the pre-test and post-test were normally distributed, as assessed by Shapiro-Wilk's test ($p=.301$). Hence, a paired sample t-test was performed to compare the self-esteem scores before and after art therapy intervention with the app.

Table 6

Paired Sample t-test Results: Mean, SD, t-value, df, r and d of paired differences between pre-test and post-test of self-esteem

	Pre-test M	Post-test M	Pre-test SD	Post-test SD	t	df	r	d
Outcome	11.00	18.50	2.83	2.39	11.28*	15	.49	2.82

*$P<0.01$

Table 6 indicated that there was a statistically significant difference in self-esteem scores before and after art therapy intervention using the app, $t(15)=11.28$, $p=0$, $r=.49$, $d=2.82$. Self-esteem increased by an average of about 7.5 points after the art therapy intervention. The effect size for this study ($d=2.82$) was found to exceed Cohen's convention ($d=.80$) for a large effect (Cohen, 1988). According to Sawilowsky (2009), the effect size of this study is huge because it is larger than 2.0. The results suggested that art therapy using the app was effective in enhancing the self-esteem of children with various problems in a school setting.

The Results of Intervention for Each Session

The School counselors recorded drawings of children with comments for each session after each session on the app. This was used to support the results of the pre- and post-test to enhance self-esteem, the results were compared with counselors' reports, and the interpretations of the researcher were reviewed by the art therapist who supervised the intervention.

Table 7

Session one

	Contents
Topic	Introduction: 'Art About Me' Free drawing
Goals	Client becomes familiar with the art therapy app through free drawing. In the warm atmosphere, he/she expresses his/her emotion and thoughts.
Drawings	D 
	E 

Children's comments	•	D: "I drew myself as a goalkeeper. I was excited because the teacher (counselor) listened to me with patience."
	•	E: "I was a bit nervous while drawing on the tablet because I haven't experienced drawing on a tablet. I was little bit afraid of using a digital device for the first time. But I became better after seeing the images that I made and satisfied with my work."
	•	H: "I was surprised to get a tablet for drawing in the therapy session. I was excited to use it. I had never expected to get a chance to use the teacher's tab at school or counseling session."
	•	O: "I drew the emotions that I usually feel. I was careful to use the app. Thank you teacher for letting me use the tablet."
School counselor's evaluation / Analysis	•	The children took some time to get familiar with the app, but they were able to understand how to use it very soon and could do well as it was free drawing.
	•	Using the app made them feel comfortable and excited and helped to build rapport. Children were able to open up mind from the first session and didn't hesitate to talk to counselor compare to verbal counselling. It helped

counselors easily understand their clients.

Session one was designed to help children get familiar with the app. Children were allowed to draw anything they wanted to draw. Three children reported that it was not easy to understand how to use the tab in the beginning. But most of the children were excited to draw on the tablet and opened up to the counselors very fast. Counselors also reported that using the app in the session helped to build rapport with the children in a short time.

Table 8

Session two

	Contents
Topic	Self-portrait
Goals	Goals include enhancing self-awareness and self-esteem by the exploration of self, facial expression, emotion, and understanding of his/her interests, personality, strength, and weakness. Using a camera and emotion stickers of the app, clients take a selfie and edit it.
Drawings	A
	B

	F	
	G	
Children's comments		• A : "I was happy to take selfies and to strike a nice pose. I wanted to make myself on the tablet have a fair complexion while editing my picture." • B : "I felt strange to take my selfies. But I felt good after decorating my picture." • F : "I was happy in this session. I was excited to take selfies and to see my pictures." • G : "I was happy to see me on the tab and enjoyed decorating my pictures."
School counselor's evaluation / Analysis		• Children were happy to take a selfie. • A opened up to a counselor and talked about his appearance in a good mood. • B was very shy while taking her picture as she thought she is not beautiful. • Some children showed their inferiority about their photos. But they were able to talk about inner conflicts without hesitation. For example, 'I don't like my eyes', 'I want a fair complexion', 'I want long straight hair' etc. • They cared about how they looked and wanted to choose a better one. When they edited pictures, they felt happier.

> Naturally, they were able to discuss how they could become a better person while decorating their pictures.
> - It was effective for children to talk about their strengths and weaknesses.

In the second session, children took photos of them and edited it with stickers, drawings, and frames. Counselors reported that children were able to open up their inferiority and inner conflicts without hesitation. Counselors could understand them well and deal with their problems. This session provided good opportunities for children to think about their hopes, characteristics, interests, strengths, and weaknesses. Children were able to take several pictures and choose the best image that they wanted to edit. They didn't worry about their mistakes and felt free to edit until they were satisfied with their work. They were comfortable making changes to their work. They gained a sense of control by choosing pictures and changing their work. It made them more confident and satisfied with their artwork.

Table 9

Session three

	Contents
Topic	Body scan
Goals	Learning how to relax the body, understanding the beauty of the body and appreciating the body.
Drawings	C

I

N

P

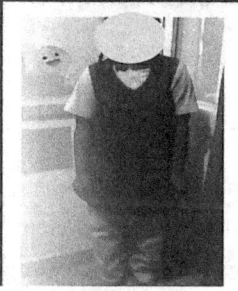

| Children's comments | - C : "I love sunshine. I want to fill my life with beautiful colors. I like the sunshine effect on my picture."
- I : "I enjoyed taking pictures and took selfies several times until I liked. I wanted to choose the best picture and liked decorating it with stickers."
- N : "I felt calm and relaxed during the session."
- P : "I became much comfortable to express my feelings. Actually, I was quite shy to talk to someone before." |
|---|---|

School counselor's evaluation / Analysis	<ul><li>It was very effective for clients to relax.</li><li>It helped them think and feel their emotions and learn how to love themselves.</li><li>It helped them to reduce their shyness gradually and to have a positive body image.</li><li>They were excited, motivated, and confident when they edited the photos to make them look better. It seemed they could relate it with themselves to change to a better person.</li></ul>

In the third session, counselors started reporting clients' confidence, motivation, and positivity about their artwork and themselves. Children were more relaxed, and they expressed more honest feelings because they were able to do their artwork with ease. Children were motivated when they edited their pictures and showed more confidence in themselves. They started to believe they can be a better person when they edited the images for them to look better. They were able to get satisfactory outputs while drawing and editing pictures without specific art skills. It made them feel good and be positive about their artwork and their body.

Table 10

Session four

	Contents
Topic	Draw myself as a superhero
Goals	Enhancing self-awareness and self-esteem by exploring his/her strengths.
Drawings	A

E

G

H

Children's comments	<ul><li>A : "I felt lonely when I started drawing, but I feel ok now, because he has power."</li><li>E : "I was happy to draw a superwoman, because she can help her friends and protect them."</li><li>G : "I drew an Iron man who has the power to help others. I know some similarities between Iron man and me. Iron man can make models with metals and I can make models with clay. We all wear glasses. I feel I can also help others just like Iron man."</li><li>H : "I drew a character called Sinchan with my favorite colors. I wanted to make others laugh through my jokes like him."</li></ul>

School counselor's evaluation / Analysis	• This was the best part of the intervention, where the students discussed their role models. • This activity made them feel more motivated and happier. • They were able to identify their good qualities to make others happy. • Some children related the superheroes to their parents, teachers, or football players who gave them more confidence.

Session four provided good opportunities for children to think about their good qualities. They were able to reflect on their strengths, such as their willingness to help others like superheroes. Moreover, they thought of how they spread happiness and how they help others. They became more confident and motivated.

Table 11

Session five

	Contents
Topic	The happiest moment & saddest moment
Goals	Awareness of the factors that impact life and learning how to balance the good and bad that they face.
Drawings	C
	D

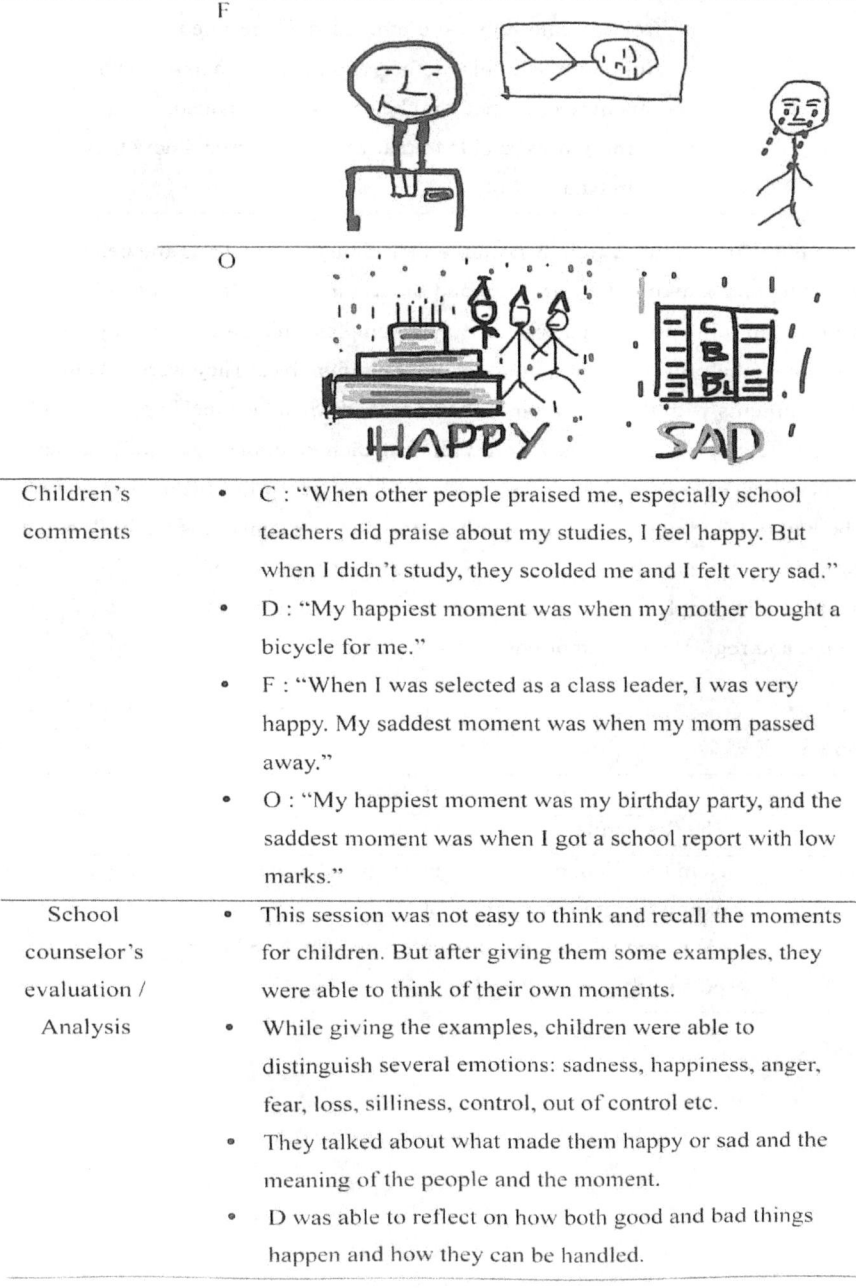

Children's comments	• C : "When other people praised me, especially school teachers did praise about my studies, I feel happy. But when I didn't study, they scolded me and I felt very sad." • D : "My happiest moment was when my mother bought a bicycle for me." • F : "When I was selected as a class leader, I was very happy. My saddest moment was when my mom passed away." • O : "My happiest moment was my birthday party, and the saddest moment was when I got a school report with low marks."
School counselor's evaluation / Analysis	• This session was not easy to think and recall the moments for children. But after giving them some examples, they were able to think of their own moments. • While giving the examples, children were able to distinguish several emotions: sadness, happiness, anger, fear, loss, silliness, control, out of control etc. • They talked about what made them happy or sad and the meaning of the people and the moment. • D was able to reflect on how both good and bad things happen and how they can be handled.

	• While drawing the saddest moment, F felt sad, and the related emotions were processed. He recalled good moments with his mother, and his good memories with his mother helped him be calm and motivated.
	• Children were able to realize and understand how they can balance both.

In the fifth session, children explored their thoughts, emotions and behaviors while thinking and drawing their happiest and saddest moments. It was not easy for some children to think about their lives deeply. Examples which were given by the counselors were helpful for them to think about their own lives. They were able to relate the moments with their emotions and understand when they feel happy and sad clearly. They talked about how they would regulate their emotions, especially sadness, and balance their life well. When F remembered the moment when his mother passed away, he had to face intense feelings. But he was able to remember his mother's smile and appreciate all the moments with her. He became more motivated to see the positive things in people. Over the course of the session, children were able to understand and regulate their emotions.

Table 12

Session six

	Contents
Topic	The first smile
Goals	Help the client remember the person who showed hospitality and express appreciation to people.
	Goals include learning to appreciate people and having a positive perspective to see the world.

DEVELOPMENT AND EFFECTIVENESS OF AN ART THERAPY APP 49

Drawings	J	
	K	
	L	
	M	
Children's comments		• J : "I drew my friend 'Z'. who made me smile and happy. I am thankful to Z." • K : "I drew my mother, who made me smile."

	• L : "I drew my uncle, I am really proud of him. I want to be a person like my uncle. He has successes in his career." • M : "I drew my mother who made me smile. When I think about her smile, I always feel confident."
School counselor's evaluation / Analysis	• This was very effective for children to think of not only their parents but also their peers whom they consider as important support for all that they do. • Children learned how to appreciate even small things that made them feel good. • Children were able to value their friendship and family love.

In this session, children had opportunities to think about people who showed hospitality to them. It was reported that they felt warmth and gratitude and had a good chance to express their appreciation. It helped them see the world positively and optimistically. Moreover, children wanted to be someone who would be nice to others.

Table 13

Session seven

	Contents
Topic	Yourself in the future
Goals	Giving opportunities to think of self in a positive and detailed manner. While hoping for the future, intervention is terminated.
Drawings	C

D

F

G

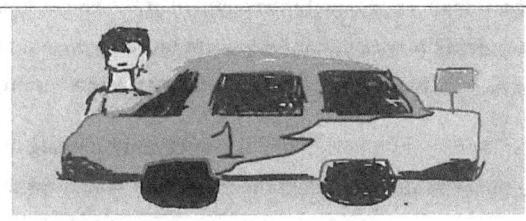

Children's comments	<ul><li>C : "I want to be a good teacher who is kind and love students."</li><li>D : "I enjoyed drawing my future. I want to be a football player or an army man in the future."</li><li>F : "I drew myself as a scientist who will invent valuable things for people."</li><li>G : "I want to become a famous cartoonist when I am 20 years old. I will become famous and own a very good car."</li></ul>
School counselor's evaluation / Analysis	<ul><li>D understood and reported how qualities and hard work would be more important than good looks to achieve his goals.</li><li>Children didn't worry about their drawing skills. They</li></ul>

were able to focus on the contents of their work.
- For a few children, it was not easy to think about their future. They said they didn't think about it in detail before. It gave them opportunities to think about their dreams, and to explore what kind of person they want to be or jobs that they can have in the future.
- This helped children look at themselves positively and confidently.
- Children became more motivated and confident about their future.

The last session was designed to terminate the art therapy intervention and for giving hope, motivation, and confidence. While thinking and drawing their future, children became more confident and motivated by their ambition. They were able to think about their good capabilities and what they have to make efforts for their future. For example, D reported that there were more important things than good appearance. With hope, confidence, and pride, art therapy intervention was terminated.

Counselors reported that the intervention using the app was effective to prepare the session, to conduct the intervention, and for documentation. They were willing to use the app in further sessions after the study.

General Impression of the App from the School Counselors

From the beginning of the workshop, school counselors were interested in art therapy, and they had a passion to know more about art therapy. They were members of a psychotherapeutic center and worked at different schools in Bengaluru, India, to provide psychological service systemically to school children. They were counselors at three different schools with English medium education. The school counselors and teachers cooperated closely to support students. The teachers and school counselor team figured out the presenting feelings of students who were referred to them, and those feelings were closely related to low self-esteem. To deal with various issues and emotions of students, the art therapy program was designed to improve self-esteem, which in turn would help reduce psychological problems. Counselors agreed to the plan and participated in the two-day workshop.

Due to the absence of art therapist training courses in India, certified art therapists were not able to participate in this study. Instead, school counselors who were eager to understand and know the basics of art therapy and use it in their counseling sessions took part. The counselors had already realized the power of art in their counseling sessions especially with children. When their clients were hesitant to talk or showed discrepancies, counselors had asked them to draw. Counselors were already using art to resolve the conflicts and to listen to clients' stories. They were interested in art therapy using the digital device because they also agreed on the limitations of using art materials in school settings. In their settings, only pieces of paper from notebooks, pencils, and a few colors were available. Even though they understood the effects of art in counseling, it was difficult to procure various art media such as papers, color pencils, watercolors, and clay for regular sessions.

During the workshop, basics of art therapy was introduced, and tablet pcs were given to them to learn how to use them. They practiced installing the app, creating accounts, drawing and editing, making journals, and backing up. They gave feedback about the app, and the app was modified based on that (table 3).

In phase three, after providing art therapy intervention to improve children's self-esteem in a school setting, they gave general feedback about the app, 'Art about Me.'

- Using the app in the session was very useful in building a therapeutic relationship with children. New media made children excited and open-minded.

- Ease of use of the app and being free to choose the element on their work empowered children and gave them confidence and motivation.

- In the beginning, some children were nervous about learning how to use a new digital device, but they became familiar with it quickly.

- Children didn't worry about their art skills for the activity. They felt free to draw, erase, and express again. It made them feel more comfortable to express themselves and focus on their story without hesitation.

- Fragileness of the tablet pc was one of the concerns among counselors. It could easily be broken when handled by children, but the children took care of it while they used it.

- It was convenient to use the app as not much preparation was required, and there was no cleaning up.

- It was easy and convenient to save images, document, and back up data. Large space for the storage of artwork and documentation was not needed.

- Counselors were willing to use this app continuously. Nowadays, most counselors use smartphones or tablet pcs. Once they download the app, the app provided an endless supply of art materials, and multiple clients can use the app. They don't need to purchase traditional art materials. From a long-term perspective, the use of the app is cost-effective.

Discussion

This chapter will discuss the usefulness of the art therapy app, "Art about Me" which was designed to satisfy the needs of art therapists and clients in art therapy interventions, this study's results, and the relationship to the literature review.

Development of an Art Therapy App, "Art about Me"

The current study developed an art therapy app to meet the needs of art therapists and clients and explore the art therapy app's effectiveness in enhancing self-esteem for children in a school setting. Existing commercial art apps did not match clients and art therapists' needs so far because they were not developed to be used in clinical settings. In this study, an art therapy app, 'Art about Me' was designed by the art therapist, with technical support provided by a developer from CDI at Christ University.

Ideal characteristics of an art therapy app, such as confidentiality, privacy, security, documentation, backing up system, ease of use, and digital accessories, were included (Choe, 2014; Matthews, Doherty, Coyle, & Sharry, 2008). For confidentiality, privacy, and security, when the app is installed, an art therapist must create his/her admin id and password to control the app. Only the art therapist who has an admin id can access clients' data, journals. Every client can create their own account under the guidance of the therapist. They can draw, take pictures, edit, and decorate with emotion stickers. They can save their work with title, comments, and date on the device. Documenting and reviewing their work are easily done under the supervision of the therapist. Digital data is saved in the device and can be exported and imported to a new device by the therapist, who has an admin ID. The interface of the app is easy for children to use. From the very first session, clients would be able to draw on the device. Digital accessories such as camera and emotion stickers have been included to enhance the quality of the work and to gain more effects.

The concern about training for therapists (Orr, 2006; Orr, 2012) was taken care of by providing art therapy workshops to school counselors. They learned the basics of art therapy and how to use the app in their sessions. At the workshop, the researcher gathered feedback about the app from participants, and the app, 'Art about Me' was modified based on it.

Effectiveness of the Art Therapy App as a medium for Art Therapy interventions for Children

To determine the effectiveness of the art therapy app "Art about Me", a self-esteem enhancement art therapy intervention was conducted on children in three different schools by three school counselors. The app "Art about Me" replaced traditional art materials.

Improvement of children's self-esteem. According to Hind and Sibbald (2015), smartphone apps were useful to reduce clinical symptoms such as stress, anxiety, depression, and improve self-efficacy. In this study, art therapy intervention using by the app "Art about Me" was given to students who were referred by class teachers because of various issues to enhance their self-esteem. Their problematic issues, as perceived by class teachers, were related to inferiority and negative feelings. Self-esteem is highly associated with psychological issues (Ateerah & Lukman, 2019; Rosenberg, Schooler & Schoenbach, 1989; Sukumaran, Vickers, Yates & Garralda, 2003). Therefore, art therapy to improve self-esteem was designed to deal with children's psychological problems

Children's self-esteem can be enhanced at schools (Hosagi, Okada, Fujii, Noguchi & Watanabe, 2012). In this study, seven sessions of art therapy intervention using the art therapy app, "Art about Me," were given to 16 children in three different schools by three different school counselors who participated in an art therapy workshop. Rosenberg's self-esteem scale was administered on the children before and after the art therapy intervention to examine the effects of art therapy using the app for children. The result of the paired sample t-test indicated that children's self-esteem was enhanced remarkably.

In session one, children experienced expressing their thoughts and emotions on the tablet with the app. For some children, it was not easy to use the digital device for drawing initially. However, they became familiar with drawing on it soon. Both school counselors and clients felt that using the app was helpful to get the children open up about their issues or problems. In sessions two and three, children had opportunities to understand their interests, personality, strength, and weakness and their body image by taking pictures based on a theme and editing with various tools.

In session four, they tried to explore their strength by comparing themselves to superheroes and thinking of how to help others with the strengths they had. In sessions five and six, children had opportunities to balance their lives, to regulate their emotions, to experience warmth from others, and to appreciate it. They could see the world positively and be good to others.

The last session was about drawing their future. They thought about their capabilities and shortcomings to grow. They became more confident and motivated for the future. This study helped children observe their deep emotions and thoughts about themselves, family, and environments and express them freely. Through the art therapy intervention, they were able to discover their strength, weakness, gratitude, hope, and motivation. It seemed that these experiences positively impacted their hope for the future in the course of the intervention. It helped them think of themselves as main actors to lead their own life. This result is in line with previous studies that art therapy is beneficial for enhancing self-esteem (Alavinezhad, Mousavi & Sohrabi, 2014; Lee, 2016; Mun & Hong, 2015).

In particular, children were able to select the elements for their artwork. The opportunities to decide what to use, what to choose, and what to change for making their best artwork without worrying about their skills were valuable for children. The creative process with artistic choices helps children to increase self-esteem and to strengthen the self (AATA, 2017; Buchalter, 2009; Thong, 2007).

Building a therapeutic alliance. The school counselors who participated in this study reported that using the app helped build a therapeutic alliance with young clients. At the beginning of the intervention, three clients were worried about using the digital device and found it challenging to use, but they learnt soon and started to enjoy it. The clients showed eagerness to learn how to use it, and they were excited to use the digital device and draw with the app. One client said, "I had never expected getting a chance to use the counselor's tab to express myself." Using the app was beyond his expectation and let him have greater expectations about the intervention. It helped the clients open up, become cooperative, and express their emotions and thoughts naturally and enthusiastically. Children also continued to experience having the power to control their work. They gained a sense of control by using the app to create their artwork, developing the therapeutic alliance between children and counselors (Choe, 2017; Thong, 2007).

Developing self-growth and potential. Art is an effective tool for children to express their feelings and thoughts (Foa, 2009; Waller, 2006). Sometimes, however, many children and adolescents experience difficulties in drawing when they think they are not good at drawing and painting. If they did not have enough chances to draw or paint before, they were worried about their artistic skills, and it wasn't easy to express and focus on themselves. While using the art app, clients didn't worry about their artistic skills because it was easy to draw and erase. After learning how to use the app and device, children didn't show hesitation and tried to draw whatever they wished without worrying about their mistakes. They could choose a picture of themselves that they wanted to edit and make it better with emotion stickers. Using the app helped enhance their autonomy and creativity to express their thoughts and feelings (Kaimal, Rattigan, Miller & Haddy, 2016).

Allowing many attempts at drawing, acceptance of mistakes, and the opportunity to make corrections helped them be relaxed, reduce shyness, and express their feelings more easily. Through these comfortable environments, it seemed that clients could experience unconditional positive regards, empathetic understanding, and congruence (Rogers, 2001). The more familiar they became with the app, the more they tried to express their image. Children could focus more on their story, be aware of themselves, and become more cooperative to solve the issues. Through the intervention, children did think about themselves, discover their feelings and thoughts, express their inner world, and hope and search for ways to solve their problems.

Easy management for counselors. Counselors also reported that they were satisfied with the ease of use, management, preparation, and documentation of the app. Usability, functionality, and accessibility are benefits for using apps in a clinical setting (Hind & Sibbald, 2014). First of all, learning how to use the app was not difficult, so clients could become familiar with the program quickly. Counselors didn't have a burden to use new media and digital software in their session. Secondly, it was easy for them to prepare and clean up the setting for art therapy intervention. When they didn't use the app, children used a piece of paper from a notebook, pencils, and only a few colors. When clients made mistakes and asked for extra materials, it was difficult to manage. The setting at school was not enough for an art activity; hence using a digital device can be a good solution. With the app, clients can experience drawing, painting, taking pictures, and editing their artwork, and counselors can document their work on the device and clean up the settings with ease. It is beneficial in resource-limited settings (Malhotra, Chakrabarti &Shah, 2019).

Throughout the intervention, children experienced understanding their thoughts, feelings, and body image in a positive way. Counselors who participated in this study also reported children showed gratitude, motivation, and confidence to be a better person, and hope for the future. The app was useful to provide effective art therapy intervention for children in a school setting, even without any specific art materials. The app replaced traditional art materials. Counselors were willing to use the app in their sessions because of the ease of preparation, documentation, and building rapport. Digital-based art therapy app holds promise for providing effective service (McLeod, 1999).

Summary and Conclusions

This chapter focuses on the major findings from the current study, and it will be followed by the limitations and implications of the study.

Art therapy is an integrative therapeutic form that is particularly effective with children in various settings. It helps to enhance self-esteem, psychological wellbeing, interpersonal skills, attention, and academic performance. Digital media is a new medium in art therapy.

In India, providing traditional art mediums such as paper, crayons and paint in rural areas and other low-income settings is difficult. On the other hand, users of computer devices and the internet are increasing rapidly. Hence, a technology-based program is one of the promising solutions to approach clients and to provide mental health services.

This study focused on two objectives.

1. To develop an art therapy application.

2. To determine the effects of art therapy using the app as a medium on the self-esteem of children in a school setting.

In phase one, the art therapy app, 'Art about Me', was designed by the art therapist and developed with a developer from CDI at Christ University. Recommended ideal characters from previous studies, such as confidentiality, privacy, security, making journal (documentation), backing up system, ease of use, and digital accessories, were developed to meet the expectations of art therapists and clients.

In phase two, an art therapy workshop was conducted for school counselors. They didn't have certification in art therapy, but they understood the effectiveness of art with children and adolescents in their practice, so they already used art in their sessions. They were given training in basic art therapy, and an introduction to the app 'Art about Me'. A manual of the intervention for improving self-esteem of children was also provided to them.

In phase three, to examine the effects of the art therapy app, three school counselors who participated in the art therapy workshop conducted art therapy for enhancing the self-esteem of children. Sixteen children between the ages of eight to fifteen were referred to them by school teachers because of bullying, academic problems, or behavioral problems at three different schools in Bengaluru.

After seven sessions of art therapy using the app, "Art about Me," their self-esteem scores statistically improved. Through the process of therapy, they showed a deeper understanding of themselves, gratitude to others, and hope for the future. School counselors who participated in this study also reported positive effects of art therapy using the app and were eager to use the app in their future sessions.

Major findings of the study

The findings of the present study are the following:

- The app, Art about Me, was managed by an administrator who was a therapist. Every client had their account and saved their artwork with their comments. Data could be accessed, exported, and imported only by an administrator. Confidentiality, privacy, security, documentation, and backing up data were the features of the app.

- A workshop for the school counselors who would give the art therapy intervention was conducted. The workshop's contents were the basics of art therapy, using the app in the session, and an art therapy program to enhance self-esteem.

- The art therapy intervention with the app 'Art about Me' significantly improved children's self-esteem in a school setting.

- Using the app was useful in building a therapeutic rapport between a therapist and a client.

- It was a valuable journey for children to develop their capacity for self-growth and the potential to solve their problems. During the sessions, they didn't need to worry about their poor drawing skills. They felt free to express their thoughts and emotions and focus on themselves. Once they focused on themselves, they could discover their problems and find hope for the future. It made them try to resolve the issues.

- The clients felt warm, comfortable, and relaxed, modifying their work whenever they wanted.

- Clients became more motivated and confident for the future.

- Counselors were willing to use the app continuously in their sessions. It was easy to prepare and manage the setting, document the client's work, and there was no need to clean up afterward.

Limitations of the Study

- There was a technical limitation for improving the backing up system and more delicate drawing.

- This study was conducted with only 16 school children. The sample size was small.

- Follow-up was not done due to the school counselors' resignation after finishing the school academic year. It was not possible to connect with the students for the follow-up.

Implications of the Study

The findings of this study provide an understanding of using digital media in an art therapy session. It was not only because of the trend but also because of practical reasons. Using computer technology in mental health services is increasing now for many reasons. But there was no app for art therapy settings, and there was a need to develop a proper app for art therapy.

To satisfy the therapeutic needs of art therapists and clients, the researcher, who is an art therapist, studied the ideal characteristics of art therapy app from the literature and developed the app, "Art about Me" with a developer from the Centre for Digital Innovation at Christ (Deemed to be University) who provided technical assistance.

This study can help art therapists and counselors across the globe. Once a therapist downloads the app on his/her device, such as a smartphone and a tablet pc, he/she can conduct art therapy in any place. After installation, an internet connection is not needed while using the app. Counselors, therapists, and practitioners can use it with ease. Especially in resource-limited settings, this would be a good solution to provide many people with mental health services. Lack of materials or loss of art materials is not a concern.

Also, it was useful for young clients to improve their psychological wellbeing and self-esteem in school settings. Children are excited to use the technical device and eager to express themselves with the app in counseling settings. Therapeutic rapport can be built fast and effectively. Specific artistic skills are not needed; young clients don't need to be concerned about their skills. They can focus on their issues and their stories effectively. They can become more cooperative to work on their problems.

- It is recommended that future research focus on the process of building a therapeutic relationship. Case study methods can be used to show how a therapeutic relationship is built.

- This research was conducted in Bengaluru, India. Art therapy using the art therapy app can be conducted in different cities and countries with different conditions to see its effectiveness.

It is hoped that this study can provide appropriate information and understanding of the art therapy app and many clients get advantages from this study.